209

To:—

From:—

THE DEVON VIHARA
ODLE COTTAGE
UPOTTERY, nr. HONITON
DEVON, EX 14 9QE
Tel 0404 891251

and with best wishes from

Tom Slack.

onsehole

TOM
作者戾洞
SLACK

Cornwall—

1992.

THODY BROS.

Also by Tom Slack:

Happy is the Day — A Spitfire Pilot's Story
Interesting things about Birds

THODY BROS.
Unusual Window Cleaners
Tom Slack

An Illustrated Children's Book for Grown-ups.
Based on Stories by James MacKenzie.

UNITED WRITERS
Cornwall

UNITED WRITERS PUBLICATIONS LTD
Ailsa, Castle Gate, Penzance, Cornwall.

All Rights Reserved. No part of this publication may be reproduced, stored in a retrieval system, or transmitted, in any form or by any means, electronic, mechanical, photocopying, recording or otherwise, without the prior permission of the Copyright owner.

British Library Cataloguing in Publication Data
Slack, Tom
Thody Bros. : unusual window cleaners.
I. Title
823'.914 [J]

ISBN 1 85200 024 4

Copyright (c) 1989 Tom Slack

Printed in Great Britain by
United Writers Publications Ltd
Cornwall

To my lovely little grandchild,
Lavinia Brennan.

CONTENTS

		Page
	Introduction	9
1	The Prothody	11
2	A Talking Robin	13
3	The Thody Brothers	15
4	A Vintage Van	17
5	A Meeting, by Appointment	19
6	Unusual Window Cleaners	21
7	Forest Wash-out	23
8	The Boardroom	25
9	More Unusual Friends	27
10	A Night at the Opera	29
11	A Career in Ruins	31
12	Local Mean Time	33
13	A Meal at the Inn	35
14	A Street in Paris	37
15	Place de la Discorde	39
16	A Curled Sandwich Machine	41
17	A Commercial Break	43
18	The Jam Roll Symphony	45
19	Bags of Hot Air	47
20	Wildlife	49
21	Airline Training Pupils	51
22	Golden Treasure	53
23	Another Night at the Opera	55
24	The Secret Treasure	57
25	The End of a Rainbow	59

INTRODUCTION

James 'Mac' MacKenzie and I joined the British American Tobacco Co. in London before the last war and after a period of Management training he was posted to Siam, now Thailand, and I was sent to Nigeria and then to Malaya, now Malaysia.

When war broke out in Europe, Mac joined the Defence Forces in Malaya, ending up a prisoner of the Japanese on the dreaded Burma Railway, and I joined the RAF in Singapore to become a Spitfire pilot in England, ending up a prisoner of the Germans.

When the war was over, the Company posted us both back to the Far East where we became good friends. However, Mac was too intelligent to find much job satisfaction in selling cigarettes in smelly native bazaars, so he asked for a transfer back to England and became the first Principle of the Company's new Management Training Centre at Chelwood in Ashdown Forest.

I was later to join the Company's Board in London, so Mac and I were able to continue seeing a lot of each other.

I persuaded the Company to turn Chelwood's extensive grounds into a Bird Sanctuary, affiliated to the Royal Society for the Protection of Birds, and Mac became its first Honorary Warden.

This is how Ashdown Forest and conservation came to play such an important part in Mac's Thody Bros. Stories.

Tom Slack, Mousehole, Cornwall. 1989

1

THE PROTHODY

If this was called a Preface you might not bother to read it and then you would never know how this book came to be written.

It is based on stories told by James 'Mac' MacKenzie to his children, Jock and Nicola, which he used to send to cheer me up when I spent some time in hospital.

He died shortly afterwards, but I know he would forgive me for simplifying some of his stories and for expanding others and introducing new ones to provide continuity with a beginning and an end.

For instance, the idea of starting with a talking robin was suggested by a friend, Martin Thorpe, who queried why every illustration included this delightful little bird, just because I happen to like birds and love robins in particular, whereas there was only a brief mention of a robin in Mac's original stories.

The book is about two unusual window cleaners named Abner, who was very tall and thin, and his little brother, Peregrine, who was very short and plump, and how they befriended someone called Mac and helped to cure him of depression by bringing a bit of fun into his life.

2

A TALKING ROBIN

Mac was a nice sensitive person who had become depressed at the sad state of the world.

He loved to walk in Ashdown Forest to forget his worries, and one evening, as he strolled up a shaded path, admiring the forest's beauty and listening to the birds, he suddenly heard a little voice high up in the trees.

"Alright, are we?" asked the voice.

"What the dickens?" said Mac in astonishment as he peered up into the branches. "Who said that?"

"Well, it wasn't the tree," said the voice "because trees can't talk."

Mac couldn't believe his ears until he saw a little robin looking down at him from a branch overhead.

"How on earth did you learn to talk?" Mac asked in amazement.

"In the same way as you," replied the robin, "by listening, but, more importantly, I am told you are depressed these days and we are here to help you."

"We?" asked Mac, "I can only see one of you."

"Yes, but I have two friends," said the robin, "I will ask them to come and visit you tomorrow to see what they can do, and I will always be around in case of need."

"But how will I know them when I see them?" asked Mac.

"You'll know them alright," said the robin, "because they are somewhat unusual." And with that he flew away into the forest.

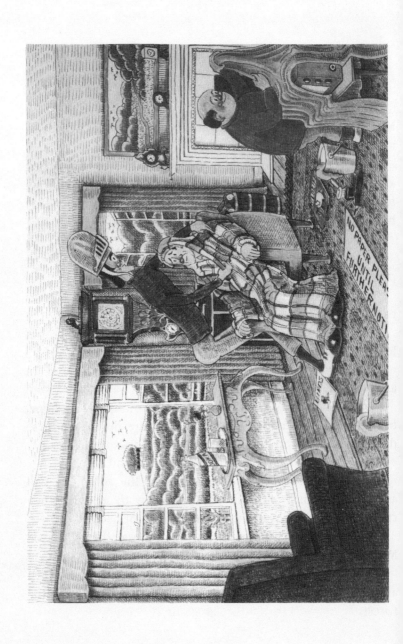

3

THE THODY BROTHERS

Mac was sitting in his favourite chair at home the next day when he heard strange voices at the window.

"Good afternoon," said a deep voice, cheerfully, "we are expected, I believe?"

Mac looked up to see two most unusual looking people peering through the window. One was very tall, wearing a strange helmet, and the other was very short, and both were carrying buckets and shammy-leathers.

"Our friend the robin sent us," said the tall one with the deep voice, "to see if we can help cure your depression, but let me start by introducing ourselves," he continued, "My name is Abner Thody and this is my little brother Peregrine, and we clean windows."

"We also help cure people who are unwell," said Peregrine, with a friendly grin, "provided they believe in us and follow our instructions."

"After hearing a talking robin and meeting you I am willing to believe in anything," said Mac, "so what do you want me to do?"

"Firstly," said Abner, as they both climbed in through the windows, "you must stop thinking of depressing things and cover up your TV set, switch off your radio, cancel your papers and wrap up well until you are cured."

"And secondly," chipped in Peregrine, "you must come and join us in the forest tomorrow to meet some of our friends and have a bit of fun."

Then the brothers were gone as suddenly as they had appeared, and Mac heard the splutter of a vehicle disappearing down the driveway.

4

A VINTAGE VAN

The Thody brothers left Mac's house and headed for the Forest in their vintage green van which they used for their window cleaning business.

They were most unusual window cleaners because Abner, being very tall, only cleaned first floor or second floor windows, and Peregrine, being very short, only cleaned basement or ground floor ones, so the windows higher up or in between were often never cleaned. This didn't seem to worry their customers who employed them more for their conversation which was legendary throughout the area.

In view of Abner's height he always wore a helmet, inherited from an ancestor, to prevent him bumping his head. This made it impossible for him to drive their van until a friend in the Royal Air Force fitted it with a war-time astrodome, which he had found lying in the corner of a hangar. The only thing missing was what the German's call a 'vind screen sveeper' to wipe away the rain, but Peregrine was always there below, at Abner's side, to guide him in emergencies.

The van, proudly displaying its conservation badge, was one of the brothers most treasured possessions, partly because of its age but also because of its magic which enabled it to take them almost anywhere, even across water.

17

5

A MEETING, BY APPOINTMENT

Abner and Peregrine had told Mac how to find them in the forest at noon the next day.

He was to head due south towards the forest until the Chanctonbury Ring disappeared below the tree line, and then he was to walk due west through the forest until his legs began to ache, when he would see an ancient, ivy-covered wall through the trees on his left. The brothers would be cleaning windows behind this wall.

Mac thought he knew every inch of the forest and had never seen or heard of such a place, but he set off in good heart to follow the instructions, waving to a robin on his garden gate as he passed, just in case it was you know who.

Sure enough, after walking for what seemed like ages his legs began to tire, and there, on his left, he saw an old wall through the trees. He followed the wall round until he came to an old iron-studded oak door which was slightly ajar, and peering through, he saw a beautiful garden and a fairy-tale castle, with the Thody brothers busy cleaning windows.

Mac went through the door and crossed a lawn to greet the brothers just as a nearby clock struck twelve.

"Welcome," said Abner and Peregrine simultaneously.

"Hello," said Mac, "and thank you for the excellent instructions."

"And thank you for being so punctual," said Abner, "because punctuality is one of The Secrets of Life, and we hope to show you many more before we've finished."

19

6

UNUSUAL WINDOW CLEANERS

Mac noticed that the brothers were cleaning the basement and first floor windows of the castle and seemed to be ignoring the ones in between. Also, he couldn't see a ladder anywhere so he wondered how the windows higher up could be cleaned.

When Mac asked about this, Abner explained politely that they only cleaned basement and first floor windows or ground floor and second floor ones.

"Isn't that a bit unusual?" asked Mac.

"We are unusual window cleaners," insisted Peregrine, with his infectious grin, "and that's how we intend to stay."

"We'll tell you a story," said Abner, "which might help make things clear."

"We once received a message from a Mrs Beryl," Abner went on, "who said she lived at the Old House, Warminghall, Bucks., and asked if we could come and do her windows."

"Before agreeing," continued Abner, "we had to check her out, because we only enjoy working for people we like and find interesting. It doesn't matter if they are poor or rich or know the Queen, we only clean their windows if they are nice and a bit unusual."

"So we went along and knocked on her door," said Peregrine, interrupting. " 'Excuse us, Ma'am,' we said, 'is this the Cold House, Warming pan, Beds?' 'If you say so,' she replied, laughing, and you must be the famous Thody brothers who have come to do my windows.' "

"How could we refuse," concluded Peregrine, "and we have been cleaning her basement and first floor windows ever since."

21

b

7

FOREST WASH-OUT

"I see you are still worried about those other windows," Abner said to Mac, placing a hand on his shoulder, "but no one else seems to worry as long as we keep up a cheerful conversation."

"Anyway, we'll be finished here in a splash," continued Abner, changing the subject, "and then we'll take you to see our Boardroom in the Forest."

"You remind us of a fair Australian friend called Dinkum," said Peregrine as they headed for the Forest, "he was more or less of average height and wanted to malligummate with us to clean those windows in between."

"You mean amalgamate," corrected Mac, politely.

"As you wish," replied Peregrine, "anyway, he wanted to call us Thody and Dinkum Limited, but who on earth wants to be limited?"

"I see the point," said Mac, "but why don't you send out a press release to explain everything to everyone?"

"A brilliant idea," said Abner, with enthusiasm, "provided you help us draft something suitable."

As they continued on their way, they suddenly came to a clearing on the edge of the Forest where a buxom woman was washing clothes and singing away about fleas and waving corn, with a slim little girl standing nearby hanging out washing on a line.

"Let me introduce you to our friend Olga Pilsudski," said Abner, calmly, as if nothing was unusual, "she is Russian and this is her charming assistant Miss Fairy Snow."

"Perhaps we should malligummate with them," said Peregrine, grinning, "with us washing windows and talking ten to the dozen while they wash clothes and sing!"

23

8

THE BOARDROOM

The brothers headed back into the Forest again, followed by Mac who gave Olga and Fairy Snow a shy little wave as he passed them by.

Before long they reached another clearing where Mac could see a wooden hut with a girl typing away furiously outside.

After introducing the typist as Penny, from Heaven, the brothers led Mac into the hut and invited him to sit at the head of their Boardroom Table.

Abner poured out drinks while Peregrine emptied the contents of his pockets onto the table, and then Abner handed Mac a sheet of paper and said, in true directorial style, "Please write the press release on that when you have decided what you want to say."

"The shorter the release the longer it takes to prepare," said Mac, "but let's head it 'PRESS RELEASE' for a start, and give me a little time to work out what should follow," he added, searching the ceiling desperately for inspiration.

"Right," said Mac, after several minutes concentration, "I'll read what I've written to see what you think. 'PRESS RELEASE'," he read, " 'THODY BROS. A STATEMENT'. 'QUOTE'," he continued, " 'Relief swept through the Forest when the THODY brothers confirmed they would never amalgamate with anyone, following rumours of take-over bids which they have firmly rejected because they want to remain their unusual selves. When asked how it felt to be unusual they said it felt fine, UNQUOTE'."

"Terrific," said Abner, in absolute admiration, "And no long words to look up in a Dictionary," added Peregrine, calling Penny to type the Statement for immediate release.

25

9

MORE UNUSUAL FRIENDS

"Well done, Mac," said Abner, beaming with delight, "that release was a masterpiece. You have earned a reward so would you like to come and meet more of our friends in the Forest?"

"You bet," said Mac, excitedly, "I've never had such fun since childhood."

"Ah, good old childhood," said Peregrine, wistfully, "all fun and games with few problems, but it can be just the same for grown-ups if you give life half a chance."

"Anyway, Mac, you seem to be coping all right," said Abner as he led Mac to the green van parked among the trees, bowing low to Penny as they passed.

"Some of our friends are a bit shy of strangers," he said, helping Mac into the back of the van, "so we hope you won't mind remaining hidden in the van on this visit while we explain who you are."

As the van rumbled along the Forest tracks, with Abner at the wheel and Mac crouched in the back, Peregrine began searching through a well-thumbed list of customers to select someone suitable for a visit.

"Let's start with Mr Chatterjee," he suggested after considerable thought, "he lives at Curry Cot and talks a lot, and we are due to clean his windows this week anyway."

"Excellent," said Abner, "and if Mac doesn't mind waiting a few extra minutes, we can cross the road afterwards to have a chat with Beniamino Trevato, the famous Italian Tenor who sings a lot and is sponsored by a Grand Duchess of Somewhere or other.

10

A NIGHT AT THE OPERA

When Abner and Peregrine had finished cleaning Mr Chatterjee's windows they said their fond farewells to him and his sacred cow, and then crossed over the road to have a chat with Signor Trevata.

"Our Italian friend was very interested to hear all about you," said Abner when they returned to the van, "and he has given you a complimentary ticket for tonight's Opera where we are due to help the Grand Duchess with the stage effects for his final number, Singing in the Rain."

"Can you come?" asked Abner, "and what do you think of our friends?"

"You bet," Mac replied, "I love opera, and I think your friends look super and most unusual, but why are so many of them foreigners?" he asked.

"We prefer to call them visitors," said Abner, "and it's fun chatting with them in different languages."

"Most of our customers are obviously locals," chipped in Peregrine, "but visitors help to add a bit of spice to life with their unusual names like Chaterjee, and then there are others like Herr von de Barr, Sayonara Arigato, Mein Herr Stepp and the Tunku Udang of Laut from Malaysia and so on."

Mac wanted to ask about the Tunku but by now they had arrived at the Opera House where Abner parked the van outside the main entrance where a space appeared to be reserved permanently for them.

They showed Mac to his seat in the front of the stalls before hurrying off back stage to carry out their important duties.

11

A CAREER IN RUINS

Beniamino Trevato's rendering of 'Singing in the Rain' was fantastic and earned him a standing ovation with a dozen or more encores, much to the distress of the orchestra, whose clothes and instruments had become absolutely drenched.

After the final curtain call, Abner and Peregrine came from back stage to collect Mac and take him home.

"Well," asked Peregrine, "what did you think of the show?"

"Incredible," said Mac, "and you were both unbelievable, but I am soaked to the skin."

"Never mind," said Peregrine, sympathetically, "We'll hurry you home so you can dry out and have a good night's rest."

On the way back, the brothers chatted away happily and told Mac about their friend Klopski whose life, they said, was also in ruins like his own.

"Klopski works in a cellar in Paris, making ruins by Appointment," explained Peregrine. "He was trained at Stonehenge and grows his own medieval grass to fill in any cracks to make his work authentic."

"Go on," interrupted Mac, "by Appointment to whom?" he asked.

"By Appointment to whoever wants to buy a ruin, of course," Abner replied, a trifle impatiently.

"Honestly," said Mac, laughing, "you'll be telling me next he comes from Thody Arabia."

"Certainly not," answered Abner abruptly. "He's a Pole, and a Pole with a problem because he has to work at night so no one will ever see him creating his ruins."

At that moment they arrived at Mac's house and after bidding him a friendly good-night they said they would be back to see him at around noon the next day.

12

LOCAL MEAN TIME

Mac heard the van approaching up the drive on the following day, and, sure enough, as punctual as ever, Abner and Peregrine appeared at his windows shortly before noon.

After the customary greetings, Mac saw them studying the various clocks in his living-room with considerable interest, and, after whispering among themselves, Abner finally decided to speak.

"We notice you appear to collect clocks," he said, "but they all show different times so how on earth can you tell the correct time?" he asked.

"Well," said Mac, "I happen to love clocks and I tell the time by . . . " but before he could finish his sentence he was interrupted by Peregrine.

"I know," burbled Peregrine, excitedly, "you take all the clocks, add their times together, and divide the total by the number of clocks."

"I do?" said Mac slowly, trying to think quickly.

"Yes," continued Peregrine, "which is surely the meaning of Mean Time anyway, and I've made a quick calculation and I make the time exactly five to twelve."

"Actually," corrected Mac, looking at his wrist watch, "it is exactly five minutes past," but as he spoke the local Church clock struck a resounding twelve.

"You see what I mean about Mean Time," said Peregrine, with obvious delight.

"We knew there must be something unusual about you," said Abner, affectionately, "to make us take to you so quickly, so let's all go off into the forest again to see what's in store for us this afternoon."

33

13

A MEAL AT THE INN

After they had left Mac's house, Abner stopped at a glade in the forest and suggested they sat under a tree for a while to admire the wonders of nature.

When they had settled down comfortably on a cushion of grass Mac asked if he could ask a question.

"You already have," said Peregrine, grinning, "but by all means ask another."

"Well!" said Mac, "it's about the Tunku Udang of Laut you mentioned. I once worked in Malaysia," he continued, "and I happen to know that a Tunku is the son of a Malay king, and Udang means prawn, and Laut means sea, so the Tunku is the Son of a King Prawn of the Sea which I find rather hard to swallow."

"Talking of food," said Peregrine, changing the subject, "we once met a French Journalist called Monsieur Scoopy Doux in the Earwig Inn at Scunthorpe who used to bow and say Bon Appetit each time he came to the dining room table."

"We used to bow back and say 'Thody'," continued Peregrine, "until the Head Waiter explained what Bon Appetit actually meant, so the next time our friend came to the table we both stood up, bowed, and said Bon Appetit in our very best French."

"And what do you think our friend said?" asked Abner, shaking with laughter.

"I haven't the faintest idea," Mac replied.

"He said Thody," said Abner, still laughing, "and the three of us kept bowing and repeating ourselves until the Head Waiter got fed up and told us to sit down and get on with our meal."

14

A STREET IN PARIS

"Monsieur Scoopy Doux became a great friend of ours," said Peregrine, "and it was he who introduced us to Klopski and lots of other unusual people in Paris."

"One of our favourite places over there," continued Peregrine, "is a little hotel in a back street off the Rue St. Antoine because all sorts of interesting people live or work nearby."

"You may have noticed we painted this Parisian scene on the back-drop for Signor Trevato's final number at the Opera," Abner added.

"I am afraid I hadn't," confessed Mac, "although I seem to remember it now, but please tell me about those people in Paris."

"All right," said Abner, "there's Henrietta who runs the dairy and sells scrumptious smelly cheeses, and the much respected Anna Marie who earns a living selling English parsnips from a Cockney barrow, and Monsieur Daniel who makes expensive Italian shirts to sell to Russian Diplomats, and the nice little lady who sits outside the Hotel selling exotic Egyptian scent which she creates and bottles herself in her cellar."

"And," interrupted Peregrine, who was beginning to feel left out of the conversation, "there's Ivor Rees who plays Chopin in his attic all day and night, and Leon Hart, the gallant mouse-trainer from Montmatre, and dear old Maitre Plas who thinks he is the reincarnation of Louis XIV and insists on being treated like royalty."

"And," said Abner, determined to have the last word, "don't forget the French Poodle which does puddles everywhere, and the chic little robin which talks with a quaint Parisian accent."

15

PLACE DE LA DISCORDE

Mac was thoroughly enjoying himself listening to the brothers talking about those unusual friends.

"When you visit France," he asked, "do you travel in your famous green van?"

"But of course," replied Peregrine, "our van can take us anywhere, even across water, but when we visit Paris we never take it inside the City itself."

"Why ever not?" asked Mac, hoping to keep them talking for as long as possible.

"Well," said Peregrine, "you know how crazy the drivers are in Paris and how they love speeding and ignore all the rules of the road, and if you have an accident," he went on, "everyone pretends to speak only French and visitors usually end up in the wrong."

"Once we were involved in a head-on collision in Paris," said Abner, "between two local Taxis careering at speed in opposite directions round the Place de la Concorde. You should have heard the two French drivers calling each other insulting names, like Tete de lard or fat head, and when a gendarme came along to keep the peace he only made matters worse."

"Paris is full of excitement," said Peregrine, giving Mac a knowing wink, "so it's a shame the French and the British can't seem to get on together."

"It seems they don't trust each other," said Abner, somewhat sadly, "and to make matters worse the French resent us because English has become a universal language instead of their own."

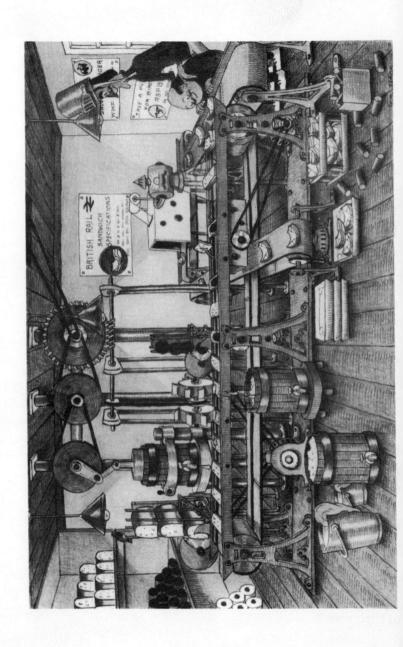

16

A CURLED SANDWICH MACHINE

The next day, when the brothers came to collect Mac, Abner suddenly burst into song as they walked together towards the green van.

"Shatzhäuser im grünen Tannenwald, Sind schon Viel' hundert Jahre alt," he sang in his very deep voice.

"Sounds like German," said Mac, "but what does it mean?" he asked.

"Roughly translated," replied Abner, "it says there is a treasure in the forest which we have been guarding for a hundred years or so."

"Is there and have you?" asked Mac, excitedly.

"Yes," said Abner, "it's a song written for us a long time ago, and sometimes I suddenly get the urge to sing it."

"But are you really a hundred years old?" Mac asked, unbelievingly, "and what's all this about a treasure?"

"You are as old or as young as you want to be," insisted Abner, looking down at Mac affectionately. "All you need is a bit of imagination, but, come on, we must be off to show you an unusual machine we have invented."

They drove Mac to a building in the forest where they showed him an incredible creation.

"It was ordered by British Railways for their Museum," explained Abner, pressing a button to bring the contraption clanking into life, "to make curled sandwiches for the Museum's Buffet Bar because visitors expect everything to be just as it used to be in the good old days of steam."

"British Railways also insisted," added Peregrine, "that the butter should be scooped off, for economy, after it had been put on, and that the sandwiches must be delivered without being flattened under their own weight."

41

c

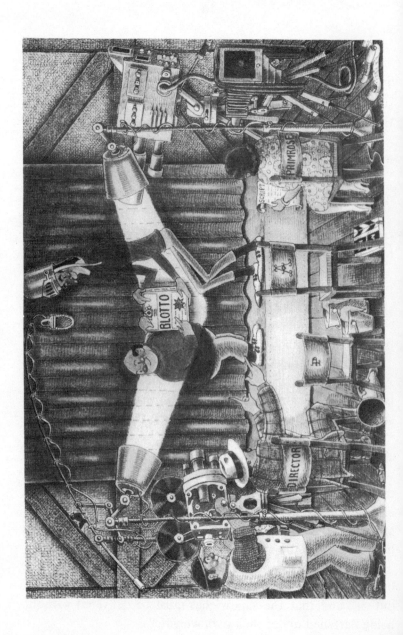

17

A COMMERCIAL BREAK

Mac thought the sandwich machine was absolutely brilliant.

"Congratulations," he said, "that's what I call real creativity."

"Creativity?" exclaimed Peregrine, "you ain't seem nuffink yet until you meet our cockney cameraman next door and his delightful lady friend."

They then led Mac to the next room where he was confronted by a stage surrounded by all sorts of cameras and equipment, with a nice looking couple waiting to greet them.

"This is where we create our Commercials," explained Abner, proudly. "Allow me to introduce you to Len Scapp, our cameraman, and Primrose, his continuity girl."

"Len insists on using old cameras," continued Abner, "because he says that anything good enough for Charlie Chaplin is good enough for him, and Primrose sees to it that every shot is spot on first time."

"One can't go wrong with friends like these, so why don't you have a go at directing?" insisted Peregrine handing Mac a stetson hat, a megaphone and a fake cigar for authenticity.

"OK," said Mac, settling down comfortably in the Director's chair, "ready, set, shoot," he shouted, and Primrose clapped her clapper-board and Len leapt into action as the brothers started to sing the praises of 'BLOTTO', the wonder cleaning powder containing magical prettipolliproppalene.

"Cut and wrap," yelled Mac, as the commercial ended, and everyone started rushing around, hugging and congratulating each other on a truly outstanding performance, and Mac now knew what it must feel like to score the winning goal in a Cup Final.

Len excitedly removed the reel from his camera and disappeared arm in arm with Primrose into the darkroom.

18

THE JAM ROLL SYMPHONY

On the way home that afternoon Mac longed to ask hundreds of questions but the brothers were in a hurry and didn't leave much time.

"I had no idea you were involved with engineering and commerce," said Mac, "Do you do all this for money or do you work for free?" he asked.

"Mostly for money, of course," replied Abner, "but we only do creative and enjoyable things otherwise work wouldn't be fun."

"And we need some money," added Peregrine, "to support the conservation of wildlife, as you must have noticed from the posters around the sandwich machine."

"I'm sorry, I hadn't noticed them," Mac apologised, "I was too interested in the machine itself."

"You appear to have discovered the secret of life," Mac went on, looking straight at Abner, "but what about that secret treasure you sang about the other day?" he asked.

Before Abner could answer they had arrived at Mac's house.

"Have some rest," Abner suggested to Mac, "and wrap up well until we come back this evening to take you to a concert where Peregrine will be performing on his Tuba-Cello."

"The Cello," said Peregrine, very seriously, "is the most beautiful of musical instruments, as everyone knows who heard that lady playing to nightingales in a wood at night, but its sound can be drowned by a full orchestra so mine is fitted with a large loudspeaker."

That night they took Mac to hear a thunderous rendering of what they insisted on calling Haydn's Jam Roll Symphony.

45

19

BAGS OF HOT AIR

When Mac went to bed that night he found it difficult to sleep thinking about the treasure and trying to imagine he was a hundred years old.

Anyway, the brothers were due to visit him again the following afternoon so he would ask them then to explain everything once and for all.

Then he fell asleep.

The brothers arrived punctually the next afternoon, and Mac invited them to stay for tea so he could have a serious talk.

They were delighted to accept, but before Mac could get in another word, Abner started on one of his reminiscences.

"Talking of commerce," he commented, ignoring Mac who was about to say that he wasn't. "We must tell you about another bright idea we have for making a bit of extra pocket-money."

"When it is cold," Abner continued, "and there is a political rally in Trafalgar Square, we set up shop on the steps of St. Martin-in-the-Fields with inflatable cushions which we fill with warm air pumped from Charing Cross Underground Station. Then we rent them," Abner went on, "for people to sit on and keep warm while listening to all that political hot air."

"Afterwards," interrupted Peregrine, not to be left out of the story, "we collect up the cushions for use on another day, and, as the warm air is free, the whole project provides us with one hundred per cent profit."

"Not bad business, eh?" beamed Abner, determined to have the last word.

20

WILDLIFE

"Talking of wildlife," said Peregrine, frowning at Mac who took the hint and decided to make no comment, "We have a friend who can talk for hours on unusual things about common birds."

"For instance," continued Peregrine, "did you know that House Sparrows are really Weaver Birds which followed the Roman Legions to Britain from the Mediterranean, and that Swifts are related to Humming-birds and not to Swallows or Martins, and that Black-headed Gulls have brown heads in summer and white ones in winter, and that Common Gulls are not common at all?"

"No, I'm afraid I didn't," said Mac, becoming quite fascinated, "so please go on."

"Well," continued Peregrine, "what looks like a bird's feet are really their toes and what looks like their knees are really their ankles, otherwise the knees would be bending the wrong way.

"Come on, Peregrine," interrupted Abner, "like our bird-watching friend you also tend to go on for hours, but you've just got time to tell Mac about our Canadian friend, Danny St. Jacques, who is a real dedicated conservationist."

At the mention of Danny, Peregrine's face lit up.

"Well," said Peregrine, "Danny lives near a frozen lake called Lac Tremblant, and he is real smart as they say over there. When he sees a plane load of hunters approaching the area he fires shots into the air to warn Old Tusky, the leader of the local wolf pack, to head for the safety of the forest followed by every form of wildlife, and when the hunters have left, Danny beats his dinner gong to bring the whole countryside back to life."

"Fancy grown up people wanting to kill living creatures for sport," concluded Peregrine, sadly.

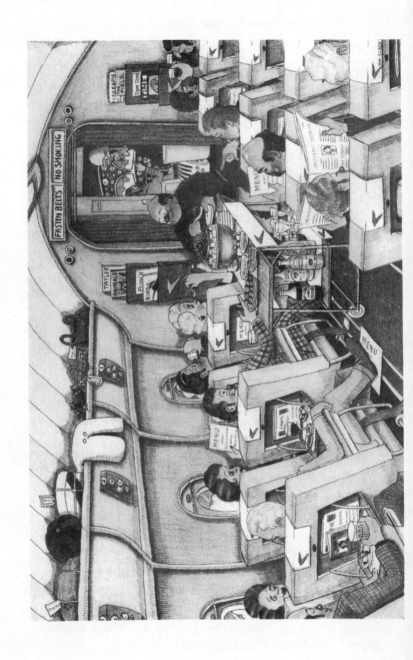

21

AIRLINE TRAINEE PUPILS

Mac was so fascinated listening to the brothers' conversation that he forgot about the questions he had decided to ask.

"Canada's a long way away," said Mac, when Peregrine had finished his story, "the fare must be rather expensive, and surely even your magic van can't cross the Atlantic?" he asked, pointedly.

"Perhaps not," said Abner, a little impatiently, "but in any case we always go there by air which is quicker and doesn't cost us a bean."

"How on earth can you fly there for free?" asked Mac.

"Well," explained Abner, "just before an Airline is due to take off for Canada I go to the pilot in the cockpit, and, saluting smartly, I tell him I am trainee pupil pilot Thody reporting for duty."

"Stiffen the crows, says the pilot," Abner continues, "not another perishing pupil pilot to plague us, and he orders me to sit in the co-pilot's seat and not to touch anything or he'll have me in irons."

"But what about Peregrine?" Mac asked.

"Please let me finish," said Abner, "once I have been accepted as air crew I go back to the entrance and beckon Peregrine to come aboard and introduce him to the cabin staff as a trainee pupil air steward."

"My job," said Peregrine, laughing, "consists of dishing out caviar and serving drinks throughout the flight, and those salty fish eggs certainly make the passengers incredibly thirsty."

51

22

GOLDEN TREASURE

The brothers often started their sentences with the word 'well', but Mac could only end his that night with "Well, well, well," after listening to this last incredible story.

After they had left, Mac sat in his favourite chair trying to concentrate about the treasure. He could kick himself now for not asking more questions, but in any case the brothers either ignored them if they were about the treasure or changed the subject, except on one occasion when they had told Mac he would jolly well have to work out the answer for himself.

Early one morning Mac had once come across some newly turned earth in the forest and thought this could possibly be the site of buried treasure until the earth began to move and a funny little face popped up and smiled at him as a mole broke the surface.

Anyway, Mac was sure the treasure couldn't be anything material like jewels and precious metal, because the brothers had told him about a trip they had once made in a Spanish Galleon in the Caribbean which was loaded with Crown Jewels, and when they had tried some of them on they found they meant nothing to them at all.

The brothers had told Mac they would be away abroad on business for a few days, so he was determined to have another go at them the moment they returned. Like them, Mac was not particularly interested in the material things of life but he hated not knowing the answer to anything.

23

ANOTHER NIGHT AT THE OPERA

The brothers called on Mac one evening a week later after returning from abroad only that same afternoon.

"You both look frightfully fit," said Mac, greeting them eagerly at his front door, "and I can't tell you how much I have missed you while you've been away."

"You look pretty fit yourself," said Peregrine, placing his hand on Mac's shoulder, "you even look as though you are just about cured and will soon be back to your former happy self."

"Also," said Abner, affectionately, "although you may have missed us, we can't be around for ever so you will have to learn how to enjoy life without us."

"I know that won't be difficult any more," said Mac, gratefully, "but can I please ask one more tiny little question?" he asked.

"Not if it's about the treasure," replied Abner, firmly, "because we have already told you this is something you must work out for yourself. It's all so simple if you use a bit of imagination," Abner added, "and when you discover the secret your heart is bound to miss a beat with excitement."

"Come along," insisted Peregrine, guiding Mac to the van, with his hand still on his shoulder, "we are going to take you to the Opera tonight as a final treat."

"Marvellous," said Mac, "I simply love Opera, as I've told you once before."

"Well," said Peregrine "this one is at Glyndebourne and it's all about the ups and downs of life and the two of us and some of our friends are performing."

"We'll be having a bit of a celebration after the show," added Abner, "so you'll be able to meet the cast and have an enjoyable evening."

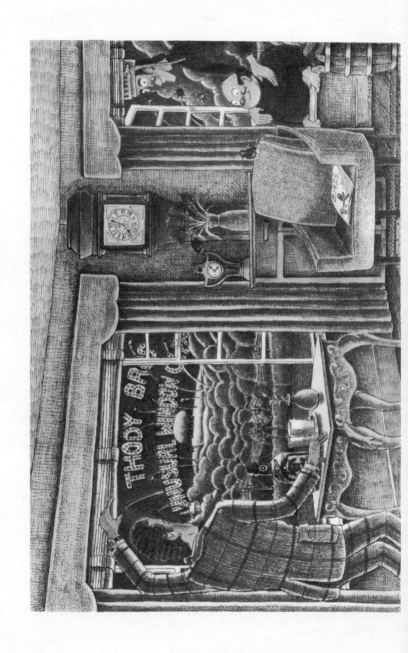

24

THE SECRET TREASURE

Mac thoroughly enjoyed the Opera and was thrilled to meet more of Abner's and Peregrine's friends.

He had not met some of those who had come all the way from Paris before, nor the three little children who apparently belonged to their friend who could talk for hours about birds.

In fact, Mac had enjoyed himself so much he slept like a top that night and felt he would never have trouble sleeping again.

The next day he felt wonderfully refreshed, and, after enjoying a large lunch, he relaxed dreamily in his favourite chair trying to solve the riddle of that elusive treasure.

He tried recalling everything about the brothers and the wonderful times they had spent together, and all the things they had said and the good advice they had given.

They obviously treasured friendship and conversation more than jewellery, and kindness and courtesy more than gold and silver, and their love of nature seemed to give them endless joy.

As these thoughts kept racing through his mind, Mac suddenly realised the full meaning of everything the brothers had been trying to tell him, so surely the secret treasure must be something to do with their secret of life.

Suddenly, Mac knew this was right because his heart missed a beat with excitement, and everything outside went dark with rockets and shooting stars bursting in all directions, spelling out Thody Bros, Unusual Window Cleaners.

Just as suddenly, the whole countryside became bathed in sunlight as Abner and Peregrine appeared at the window to wake Mac from his dream.

25

THE END OF A RAINBOW

"Congratulations," said Abner, absolutely beaming with delight, "we knew you would find the answer to the treasure in the end, but we had to let you work it out for yourself so please forgive us for appearing a bit evasive at times."

"Now that you're obviously cured," Abner continued, "why not come and join us on the terrace so we can say our fond farewells."

Mac jumped through the window, which was something he had never done before, to join them as quickly as he could.

"We can't tell you, Mac, how much we have loved meeting you," said Peregrine, wiping a tear from his eyes, "and we'll never forget the happy times we have spent together."

"That goes for me too," said Abner, his deep voice trembling a little, "so please don't ever forget the secret of life which has always been there for the asking and is all absolutely for free."

Suddenly, Mac realised this was to be a final good-bye.

"You're leaving me aren't you?" Mac asked with a lump in his throat.

"We have to," explained Abner, "we've lots of windows to clean and more people to cure. Our work is never done."

"I can't thank you enough, and the robin and all your friends too, for everything you have done for me," said Mac, with a tear running down his cheek, and, as they touched each other and said their final good-bye, a beautiful rainbow arched over them, stretching up from Mac's garden and down into the forest.

"You know what you find at the end of rainbows," said Abner, smiling as they picked up their buckets, and then they were gone.